FOR THE Best MƏM EVER

summersdale

FOR THE BEST MOM EVER

An Hachette UK Company
www.hachette.co.uk

Summersdale Publishers Ltd
Part of Octopus Publishing Group Limited
Carmelite House
50 Victoria Embankment
LONDON
EC4Y 0DZ
UK

www.summersdale.com

Printed and bound in China

ISBN: 978-1-78783-230-5

Substantial discounts on bulk quantities of Summersdale books are available to corporations, professional associations and other organizations. For details contact general enquiries: telephone: +44 (0) 1243 771107 or email: enquiries@summersdale.com

TO..............................

FROM..........................

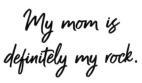

My mom is
definitely my rock.

ALICIA KEYS

Any mother could perform the jobs of several air traffic controllers with ease.

LISA ALTHER

THERE'S NO
DOUBT THAT
MOTHERHOOD IS
THE BEST THING
IN MY LIFE. IT'S
ALL THAT REALLY
MATTERS.

Courteney Cox

**Mother's love is peace.
It need not be acquired,
it need not be deserved.**

ERICH FROMM

My mother was my role model before I even knew what that word was.

LISA LESLIE

FAMILY IS NOT AN
IMPORTANT THING,
IT'S EVERYTHING.

Michael J. Fox

YOU'RE MY
*guiding
light.*

MY MOTHER'S
LOVE HAS
ALWAYS BEEN
A SUSTAINING
FORCE FOR
OUR FAMILY.

Michelle Obama

IT DOESN'T MATTER
HOW OLD YOU
ARE, OR WHAT
YOU DO IN YOUR
LIFE, YOU NEVER
STOP NEEDING
YOUR MUM.

Kate Winslet

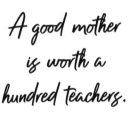

A good mother
is worth a
hundred teachers.

ITALIAN PROVERB

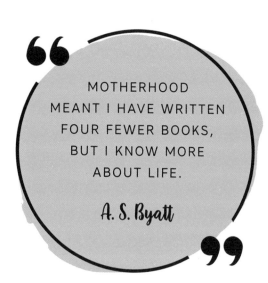

66

MOTHERHOOD
MEANT I HAVE WRITTEN
FOUR FEWER BOOKS,
BUT I KNOW MORE
ABOUT LIFE.

A. S. Byatt

99

WHEN A CHILD NEEDS
A MOTHER TO TALK TO,
NOBODY ELSE BUT A
MOTHER WILL DO.

Erica Jong

God could not be everywhere, and therefore he made mothers.

RUDYARD KIPLING

THE OLDER
I GET, THE MORE
I SEE THE POWER
OF THAT YOUNG
WOMAN, MY
MOTHER.

Sharon Olds

Spending time with YOU is my favourite thing to DO.

I LIKE IT WHEN MY
MOTHER SMILES.
AND I ESPECIALLY
LIKE IT WHEN
I MAKE HER SMILE.

Adriana Trigiani

A mother is one to whom you hurry when you are troubled.

EMILY DICKINSON

The family is one of
nature's masterpieces.

GEORGE SANTAYANA

THERE'S NO WAY TO
BE A PERFECT MOTHER,
AND A MILLION WAYS
TO BE A GOOD ONE.

Jill Churchill

Yes, Mother.
I can see you are
flawed. You have not
hidden it. That is your
greatest gift to me.

ALICE WALKER

MAMA WAS MY
GREATEST TEACHER,
A TEACHER OF
COMPASSION,
LOVE AND
FEARLESSNESS.

Stevie Wonder

IF I COULD DO HALF
AS GOOD A JOB AS
MY MOM DID, I'D
BE PRETTY HAPPY.

Jennifer Garner

You are the glue that holds everything together.

SHE IS PURE
UNCONDITIONAL
LOVE. SHE IS GRACE
AND MERCY. SHE
IS STRENGTH AND
PROTECTION. SHE
IS GIVER OF LIFE.
SHE IS A MOTHER.

Taraji P. Henson

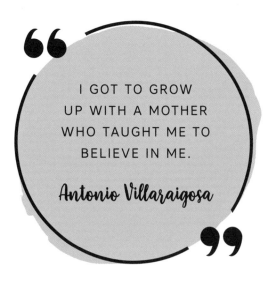

I GOT TO GROW
UP WITH A MOTHER
WHO TAUGHT ME TO
BELIEVE IN ME.

Antonio Villaraigosa

All motherly love
is really without
reason and logic.

JOAN CHEN

I WILL ACCEPT
LOTS OF THINGS,
BUT NOT WHEN
SOMEONE INSULTS
MY MUM, THE
NICEST PERSON
IN THE WORLD.

Andy Murray

If evolution really works, how come mothers only have two hands?

MILTON BERLE

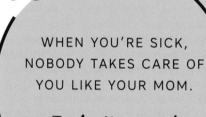

WHEN YOU'RE SICK,
NOBODY TAKES CARE OF
YOU LIKE YOUR MOM.

Trisha Yearwood

A MOTHER'S LOVE...
PERCEIVES NO
IMPOSSIBILITIES.

Cornelia Paddock

A MOTHER
CAN DO MORE
IN HALF AN
HOUR THAN
MOST PEOPLE
DO IN A
day.

SWEATER, NOUN:

GARMENT WORN

BY CHILD WHEN

ITS MOTHER IS

FEELING CHILLY.

Ambrose Bierce

**My mother has always
been my emotional
barometer and
my guidance.**

EMMA STONE

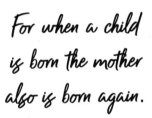

For when a child is born the mother also is born again.

GILBERT PARKER

BUT BEHIND ALL
YOUR STORIES
IS ALWAYS YOUR
MOTHER'S STORY,
FOR HERS IS WHERE
YOURS BEGINS.

Mitch Albom

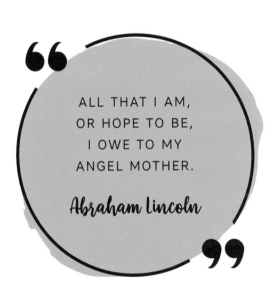

ALL THAT I AM,
OR HOPE TO BE,
I OWE TO MY
ANGEL MOTHER.

Abraham Lincoln

It takes courage to raise children.

JOHN STEINBECK

LIFE BEGAN
WITH WAKING UP
AND LOVING MY
MOTHER'S FACE.

George Eliot

All mothers are superheroes.

I AM SURE THAT IF
THE MOTHERS OF
VARIOUS NATIONS
COULD MEET,
THERE WOULD BE
NO MORE WARS.

E. M. Forster

I BELIEVE IN THE
STRENGTH AND
INTELLIGENCE
AND SENSITIVITY
OF WOMEN...
MY MUM IS
A STRONG WOMAN
AND I LOVE HER
FOR IT.

Tom Hiddleston

Moms are as relentless as the tides. They don't just drive us to practice, they drive us to greatness.

STEVE RUSHIN

WHERE THERE IS
A MOTHER IN THE
HOME, MATTERS
GO WELL.

Amos Bronson Alcott

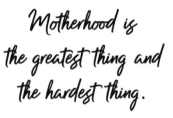

Motherhood is
the greatest thing and
the hardest thing.

RICKI LAKE

Being a mother is exhausting, but it really is the best job in the world.

SANDRA BULLOCK

MY MOTHER IS A
WALKING MIRACLE.

Leonardo DiCaprio

I APPRECIATE
everything
YOU DO
FOR ME.

A MOTHER'S LOVE
FOR HER CHILD IS LIKE
NOTHING ELSE IN
THE WORLD.

Agatha Christie

I SHALL NEVER
FORGET MY MOTHER,
FOR IT WAS SHE
WHO PLANTED AND
NURTURED THE FIRST
SEEDS OF GOOD
WITHIN ME.

Immanuel Kant

A CHILD'S FIRST
TEACHER IS
ITS MOTHER.

Peng Liyuan

WE ALL COME
FROM WOMEN, AND
THERE'S SOMETHING
EXTRAORDINARY
ABOUT THE MOTHERS
WHO RAISED US.

Annie Lennox

My mother is everything to me. She's my anchor, she's the person I go to when I need to talk to someone.

DEMI LOVATO

THERE IS NOTHING
IN THE WORLD OF
ART LIKE THE SONGS
MOTHER USED TO SING.

Billy Sunday

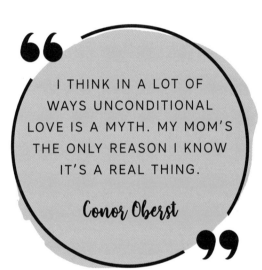

"

I THINK IN A LOT OF
WAYS UNCONDITIONAL
LOVE IS A MYTH. MY MOM'S
THE ONLY REASON I KNOW
IT'S A REAL THING.

Conor Oberst

"

YOU
ALWAYS
KNOW JUST
WHAT TO
say.

WE HAVE CHARTS, MAPS AND LISTS ON THE FRIDGE, ALL OVER THE HOUSE. I SOMETIMES FEEL LIKE I'M WITH THE CIA.

Kate Winslet

My mother's menu consisted of two choices: Take it or leave it.

BUDDY HACKETT

A MOTHER IS SHE WHO CAN TAKE THE PLACE OF ALL OTHERS BUT WHOSE PLACE NO ONE ELSE CAN TAKE.

Gaspard Mermillod

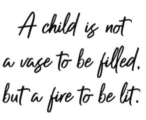

A child is not
a vase to be filled,
but a fire to be lit.

FRANÇOIS RABELAIS

You don't take a class;
you're thrown into
motherhood and learn
from experience.

JENNIE FINCH

I SUSTAIN MYSELF
WITH THE LOVE
OF FAMILY.

Maya Angelou

NO ONE PUTS HER
FAMILY FIRST LIKE MY
MOM, AND NO ONE LOVES
AND SUPPORTS ME AS
UNCONDITIONALLY AS HER.

Jenna Dewan

**I admit it –
you were right
all along!**

A mother is a person who, seeing there are only four pieces of pie for five people, promptly announces she never did care for pie.

TENNEVA JORDAN

A MOTHER KNOWS
WHAT HER CHILD'S
GONE THROUGH,
EVEN IF SHE DIDN'T
SEE IT HERSELF.

Pramoedya Ananta Toer

THE TERM
"WORKING MOTHER"
IS REDUNDANT.

Donna Reed

Biology is the least of what makes someone a mother.

OPRAH WINFREY

There is no love as pure, unconditional and strong as a mother's love.

HOPE EDELMAN

THEY SAY OUR
MOTHERS REALLY
KNOW HOW TO
PUSH OUR BUTTONS
BECAUSE THEY
INSTALLED THEM.

Robin Williams

> **I AM IN AWE OF YOUR WISDOM AND GRACE, AND I HOPE I CAN EMULATE THOSE IDEALS WITH MY OWN CHILD.**

*Jessica Biel
to her mother*

You
inspire me
EVERY
day.

MOTHERS POSSESS
A POWER BEYOND
THAT OF A KING
ON HIS THRONE.

Mabel Hale

THE MOST
IMPORTANT THING
IN THE WORLD IS
FAMILY AND LOVE.

John Wooden

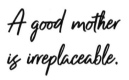

*A good mother
is irreplaceable.*

ADRIANA TRIGIANI

YOUTH FADES,
LOVE DROOPS,
THE LEAVES OF
FRIENDSHIP FALL;
A MOTHER'S SECRET
HOPE OUTLIVES
THEM ALL.

Oliver Wendell Holmes Sr

I admire her tenacity
and her generosity
and her ability to do
17 things at once.

MELISSA RIVERS
ON HER MOTHER JOAN RIVERS

WHATEVER
ELSE IS UNSURE,
A MOTHER'S
LOVE IS NOT.

James Joyce

IT MAY BE POSSIBLE
TO GILD PURE
GOLD, BUT WHO
CAN MAKE HIS
MOTHER MORE
BEAUTIFUL?

Mahatma Gandhi

I HOPE YOU
KNOW HOW
special
YOU ARE.

THE NATURAL STATE
OF MOTHERHOOD IS
UNSELFISHNESS.

Jessica Lange

In time of test, family is best.

BURMESE PROVERB

A GOOD MOTHER
LOVES FIERCELY BUT
ULTIMATELY BRINGS
UP HER CHILDREN
TO THRIVE
WITHOUT HER.

Erin Kelly

IF AT FIRST YOU
DON'T SUCCEED,
TRY DOING IT
THE WAY YOUR
MOTHER TOLD
YOU TO IN THE
BEGINNING.

Anonymous

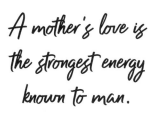

A mother's love is
the strongest energy
known to man.

JAMIE McGUIRE

Mothers give up so much, so that their children can have so much.

CATHERINE PULSIFER

ONE OF THE OLDEST
HUMAN NEEDS IS HAVING
SOMEONE TO WONDER
WHERE YOU ARE WHEN
YOU DON'T COME
HOME AT NIGHT.

Margaret Mead

YOU BRING
OUT THE
best
IN ME.

MOTHER LOVE IS
THE FUEL THAT
ENABLES A NORMAL
HUMAN BEING
TO DO THE
IMPOSSIBLE.

Marion C. Garretty

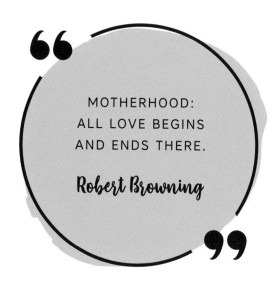

MOTHERHOOD:
ALL LOVE BEGINS
AND ENDS THERE.

Robert Browning

Our mothers always remain the strangest, craziest people we've ever met.

MARGUERITE DURAS

BEING WHO YOU
TRULY WANT TO BE
– WHO YOU TRULY
ARE – IS ONE OF THE
MOST IMPORTANT
THINGS MY MOTHER
TAUGHT ME.

Kelly Osbourne

My mother is my root, my foundation.

MICHAEL JORDAN

IT SEEMS TO ME
THAT MY MOTHER
WAS THE MOST
SPLENDID WOMAN
I EVER KNEW.

Charlie Chaplin

*Children are
the anchors of a
mother's life.*

SOPHOCLES

You light up
every room you
walk into.

WHO RAN TO HELP
ME WHEN I FELL,
AND WOULD SOME
PRETTY STORY TELL,
OR KISS THE PLACE
TO MAKE IT WELL?
MY MOTHER.

Ann Taylor

Acceptance, tolerance, bravery, compassion. These are the things my mom taught me.

LADY GAGA

SUCCESSFUL MOTHERS
ARE NOT THE ONES
THAT HAVE NEVER
STRUGGLED. THEY ARE
THE ONES THAT NEVER
GAVE UP, DESPITE
THE STRUGGLES.

Sharon Jaynes

NO GIFT TO
YOUR MOTHER
CAN EVER EQUAL
HER GIFT TO
YOU – LIFE.

Anonymous

A mother never realizes
that her children are
no longer children.

JAMES AGEE

Of all the
rights of women,
the greatest is
to be a mother.

LIN YUTANG

THE MOTHER'S
HEART IS THE CHILD'S
SCHOOLROOM.

Henry Ward Beecher

MOM IS JUST
ANOTHER
WORD FOR
home.

FOR MOST
EXHAUSTED MUMS,
THEIR IDEA OF
"WORKING OUT" IS
A GOOD, ENERGETIC
LIE-DOWN.

Kathy Lette

Mother is the one we count on for the things that matter most of all.

KATHARINE BUTLER HATHAWAY

THERE IS NO VELVET
SO SOFT AS A
MOTHER'S LAP, NO
ROSE AS LOVELY AS
HER SMILE, NO PATH
SO FLOWERY AS THAT
IMPRINTED WITH
HER FOOTSTEPS.

Edward Thomson

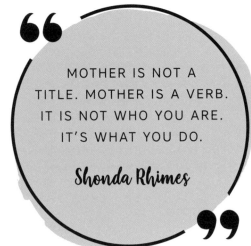

MOTHER IS NOT A
TITLE. MOTHER IS A VERB.
IT IS NOT WHO YOU ARE.
IT'S WHAT YOU DO.

Shonda Rhimes

THERE IS SUCH A
SPECIAL SWEETNESS
IN BEING ABLE TO
PARTICIPATE IN
CREATION.

Pamela S. Nadav

SHE'S INSPIRING,
SHE'S STRONG,
SHE'S FUNNY,
SHE'S CREATIVE,
SHE'S TALENTED...
SHE'S EVERYTHING
THAT I WANT TO BE.

Beyoncé on her mother

THE PATIENCE OF A
MOTHER MIGHT BE
LIKENED TO A TUBE
OF TOOTHPASTE –
IT'S NEVER QUITE
ALL GONE.

Anonymous

YOU'RE A
M♡M IN A
million.

No influence is so powerful as that of the mother.

SARAH JOSEPHA HALE

> EVERY BEETLE
> IS A GAZELLE IN
> THE EYES OF
> ITS MOTHER.
>
> *Moorish proverb*

MUM ALWAYS SAYS
THE RIGHT THING.
SHE ALWAYS MAKES
EVERYTHING BETTER.

Sophie Kinsella

**My mother's great...
She could stop you
from doing anything,
through a closed door
even, with a single look.**

WHOOPI GOLDBERG

My mother had a great deal of trouble with me, but I think she enjoyed it.

MARK TWAIN

A SMART MOTHER
MAKES OFTEN A BETTER
DIAGNOSIS THAN A
POOR DOCTOR.

August Bier

PARADISE IS
AT THE FEET OF
THE MOTHER.

Arabic proverb

THERE ARE
NO PROBLEMS
THAT MOM
CAN'T
fix.

TO A CHILD'S EAR,
"MOTHER" IS MAGIC IN
ANY LANGUAGE.

Arlene Benedict

THINK OF YOUR
MOTHER AND SMILE
FOR ALL OF THE
GOOD PRECIOUS
MOMENTS.

Ana Monnar

A mother's kiss lovingly forgives the past, present, and future.

TERRI GUILLEMETS

WHILE WE TRY TO
TEACH OUR CHILDREN
ALL ABOUT LIFE, OUR
CHILDREN TEACH US
WHAT LIFE IS
ALL ABOUT.

Angela Schwindt

I'm never going to find someone as good as my mother, am I?

JUSTIN TIMBERLAKE

Mothers always know.

OPRAH WINFREY

THERE WAS NEVER
A GREAT MAN
WHO HAD NOT A
GREAT MOTHER.

Olive Schreiner

Everything
I am,
YOU
helped me
to be.

YOU WILL ALWAYS
BE YOUR CHILD'S
FAVORITE TOY.

Vicki Lansky

Mother is the heartbeat in the home; and without her, there seems to be no heart throb.

LEROY BROWNLOW

A MOTHER
UNDERSTANDS
WHAT A CHILD
DOES NOT SAY.

Jewish proverb

A little girl, asked where
her home was, replied,
"Where mother is."

KEITH L. BROOKS

MY MOTHER IS
THE BONES OF MY
SPINE, KEEPING ME
STRAIGHT AND TRUE.
SHE IS MY BLOOD...
SHE IS THE BEATING
OF MY HEART.

Kristin Hannah

MOTHER – THAT
WAS THE BANK
WHERE WE
DEPOSITED ALL
OUR HURTS
AND WORRIES.

Thomas De Witt Talmage

PARENTING IS THE EASIEST
THING IN THE WORLD TO
HAVE AN OPINION ABOUT,
BUT THE HARDEST THING
IN THE WORLD TO DO.

Matt Walsh

YOU ARE
THE GLUE
THAT HOLDS
US ALL
together.

**To describe my mother
would be to write
about a hurricane in
its perfect power.**

MAYA ANGELOU

FAMILY IS THE
MOST IMPORTANT
THING IN THE
WORLD.

Diana, Princess of Wales

I am convinced that this is the greatest power in the universe.

N. K. JEMISIN ON MOTHERS

SHE NEVER QUITE
LEAVES HER
CHILDREN AT HOME,
EVEN WHEN SHE
DOESN'T TAKE
THEM ALONG.

Margaret Culkin Banning

A MOTHER IS
THE ONE WHO FILLS
YOUR HEART IN THE
FIRST PLACE.

Amy Tan

If love is sweet
as a flower, then
my mother is that
sweet flower of love.

STEVIE WONDER

I thought my mom's whole purpose was to be my mom. That's how she made me feel.

NATASHA GREGSON WAGNER

NO LANGUAGE
CAN EXPRESS THE
POWER AND BEAUTY
AND HEROISM
AND MAJESTY OF A
MOTHER'S LOVE.

Edwin Hubbell Chapin

I get all my
best bits
from you!

MY MOTHER
NEVER GAVE
UP ON ME.

Denzel Washington

That's the wonderful thing about mothers, you can because you must, and you just DO.

KATE WINSLET

I REALIZED WHEN YOU LOOK AT YOUR MOTHER, YOU ARE LOOKING AT THE PUREST LOVE YOU WILL EVER KNOW.

Mitch Albom

THERE IS ONLY ONE PRETTY
CHILD IN THE WORLD, AND
EVERY MOTHER HAS IT.

Chinese proverb

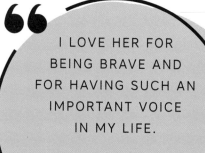

66

I LOVE HER FOR
BEING BRAVE AND
FOR HAVING SUCH AN
IMPORTANT VOICE
IN MY LIFE.

*Salma Hayek
on her mother*

99

Sing out loud in the car even, or especially, if it embarrasses your children.

MARILYN PENLAND

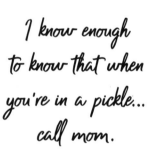

I know enough
to know that when
you're in a pickle...
call mom.

JENNIFER GARNER

You CAN fool some people, but you CAN'T fool your m♥m.

I may be a novice, but I'm learning from the best.

ALEX JONES DESCRIBING HER
MOTHER AS HER ROLE MODEL

WORKING MOTHERS
ARE GUINEA PIGS
IN A SCIENTIFIC
EXPERIMENT TO
SHOW THAT SLEEP
IS NOT NECESSARY
TO HUMAN LIFE.

Anonymous

I WONDERED IF MY
SMILE WAS AS BIG AS
HERS. MAYBE AS BIG.
BUT NOT AS BEAUTIFUL.

Benjamin Alire Sáenz
on his mother

If you're interested in finding out more about our books, find us on Facebook at **Summersdale Publishers** and follow us on Twitter at **@Summersdale.**

www.summersdale.com

Image credits

pp.1, 11, 17, 24, 30, 41, 46, 53, 69, 80, 87, 96, 102, 111, 121, 136, 140, 148 © Mariart_i/Shutterstock.com

pp.14, 28, 32, 39, 49, 57, 64, 73, 92, 110, 116, 123, 133, 143, 152 © BananyakoSensei/Shutterstock.com

pp.26, 42, 66, 98, 147 © Natalisa/Shutterstock.com

pp.34, 58, 106, 123, 138, 159 © WorkingPens/Shutterstock.com